germ SMART!

INFECTIOUS DISEASES FOR KIDS

Children's Biology Books

BABY PROFESSOR
EDUCATICN KIDS

Speedy Publishing LLC
40 E. Main St. #1156
Newark, DE 19711
www.speedypublishing.com

how come people get sick? Lots of times, it's because of the germs they pick up as they go to school, eat food, or hang out with other people. How does that happen, and what can you do to keep healthy? Let's find out.

DIFFERENT TYPES OF GERMS

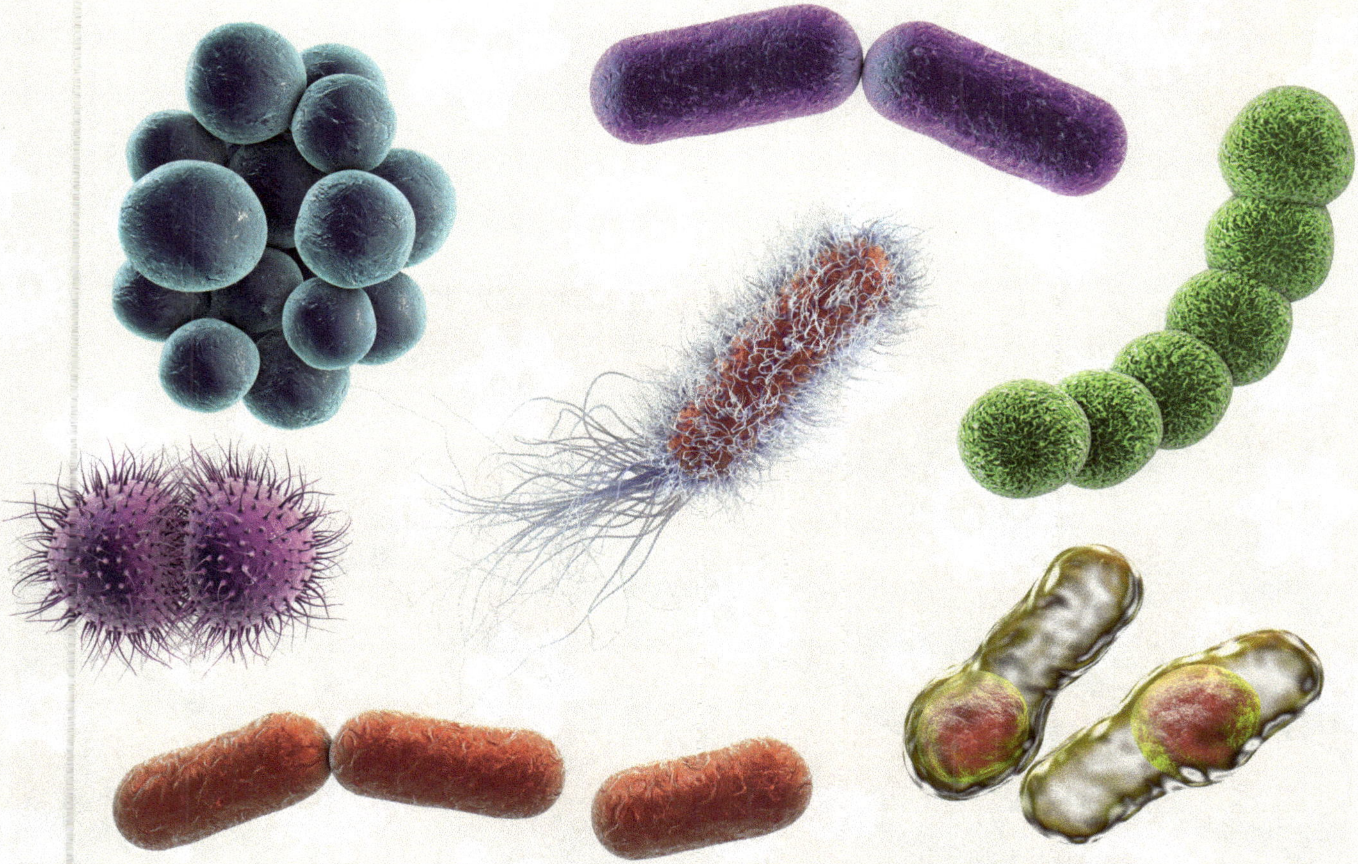

Bacteria of different shapes.

We can meet germs in several different ways, through bacteria, fungi, viruses or protozoa. Let's find out about each type of germ carrier.

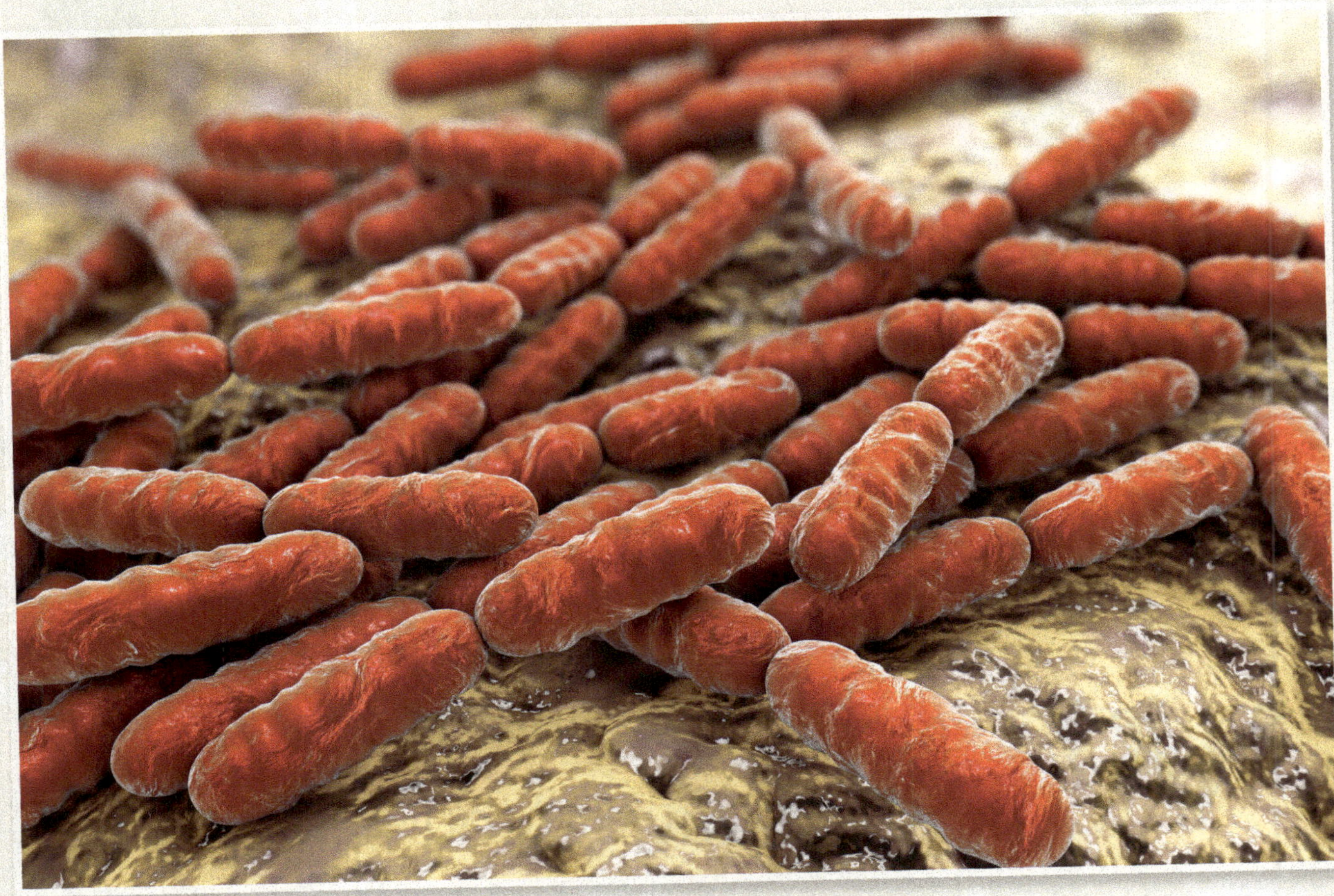

bacteria

There are good bacteria and bad bacteria. Some good bacteria live inside us and help our body do things like digest food. But bad bacteria can make us sick.

Bacteria Lactobacillus: Lactic acid bacteria which are part of normal flora of human intestine and are used as probiotics and in yoghurt production.

Bacteria survive by getting nutrients from the world around them. If they are on or in your body, they are getting their food from you. They reproduce very quickly, so once they are in your body they can increase and spread more quickly than your body can deal with.

Bacteria can cause sore throats, including tonsillitis; ear infections; cavities in our teeth; and even serious diseases like pneumonia.

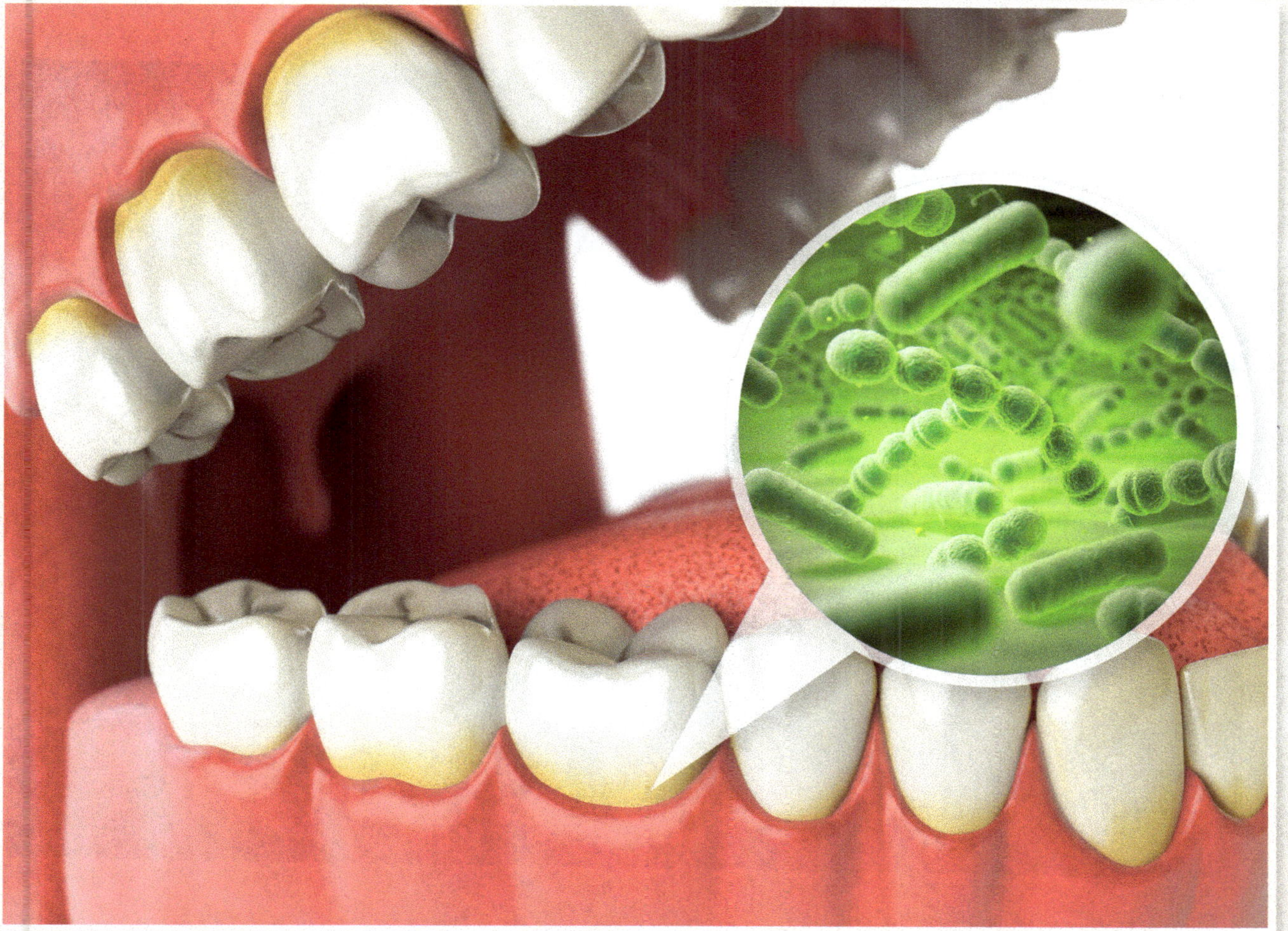

Bacterias and viruses around tooth.

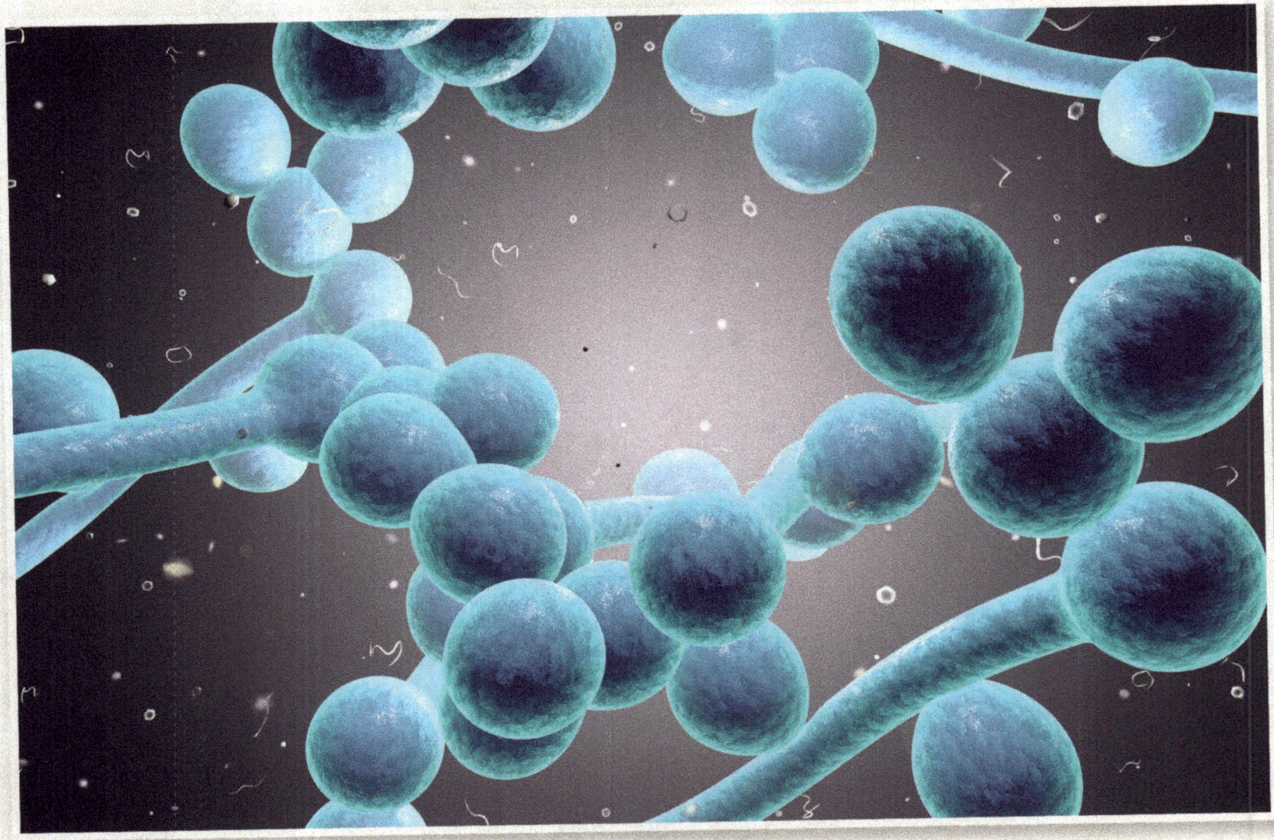

Fungi Candida albicans which cause candidiasis.

fungi

Fungi are like primitive plants, but unlike other plants they cannot make their own food. They get the nutrients they need from other plants, from animals, and maybe from you! Fungi can cause skin problems like athlete's foot and ringworm on a person.

Fungi, and its cousins mold and mildew, like warm, damp spots in your house, like under bathroom rugs or the edges of shower curtains. If you throw your sweaty socks in the closet and forget to wash them, fungi and mold will find them!

Faucet with lime deposit calcified water and tiles with fungi moisture problem.

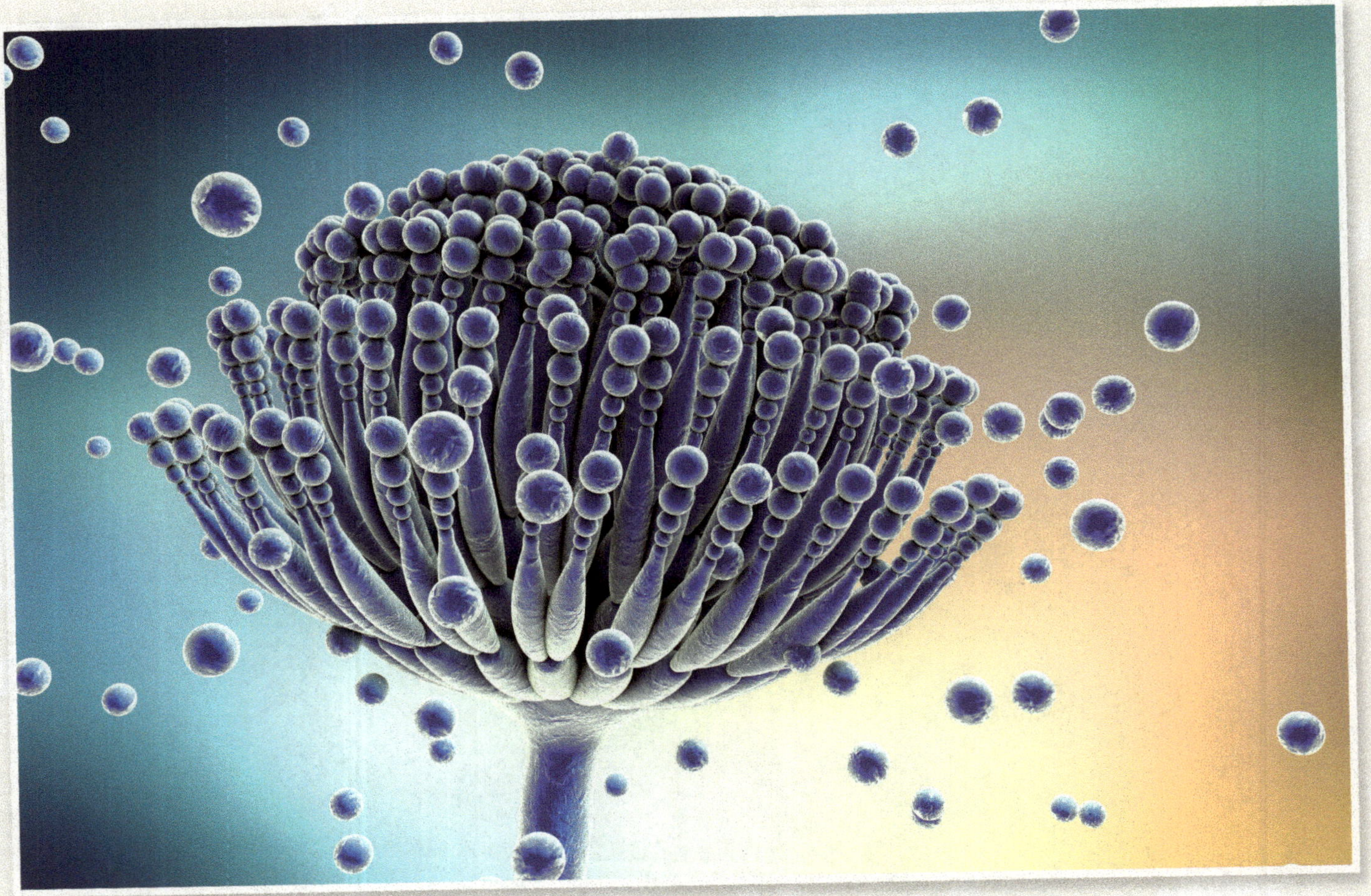

You can get sick when fungi start living on your skin, or when you breathe in some of its spores (seeds). Mold spores can cause an asthma attack or an allergic reaction.

Black mold fungi Aspergillus which produce aflatoxins and cause pulmonary infection aspergillosis.

Protozoa

Protozoa are tiny, one-celled animals. There can be thousands of them, of different kinds, in a single drop of water.

Protozoa can get into your body when you drink water that is not clean, or when you touch your lips with sweaty, dirty fingers. Some insects, like mosquitoes, can transfer protozoa to you when they bite you.

Protozoa under a microscope.

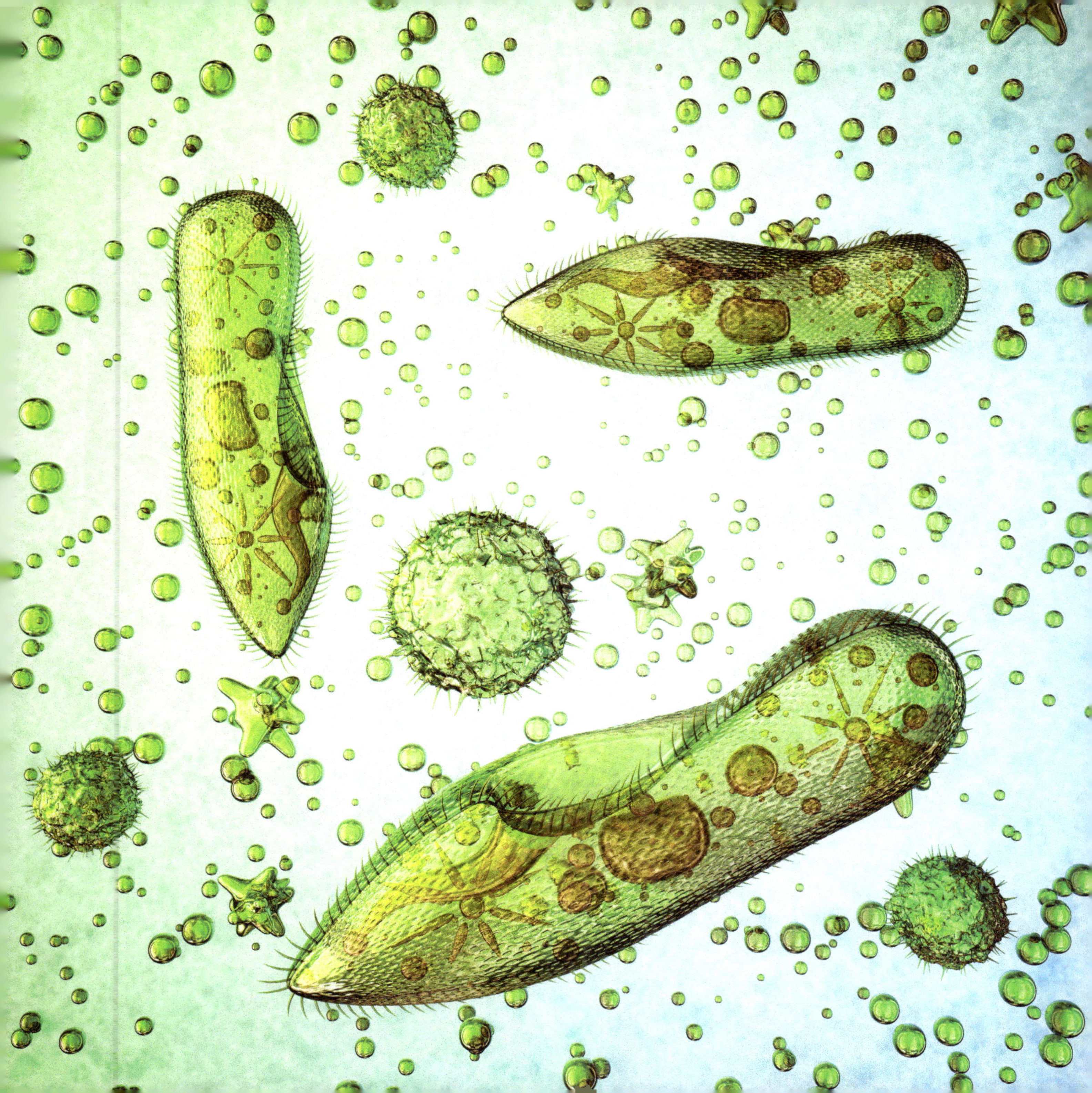

Mosquito on a human hand.

Once protozoa are in your body, they can cause all sorts of trouble: nausea, diarrhea, and severe stomach pain. They can interfere with how you digest your food. Those protozoa the mosquitoes give you can cause you to be very sick with malaria. Learn more about malaria and other serious diseases in the Baby Professor book The Deadliest Diseases in History.

viruses

Viruses are not as complicated as bacteria, but they are still dangerous. They cannot reproduce unless they are inside a plant or an animal—or you. As their "host" lives and grows, the virus multiplies and grows inside it.

Viruses can make you very sick. They can cause serious diseases like chicken pox and measles.

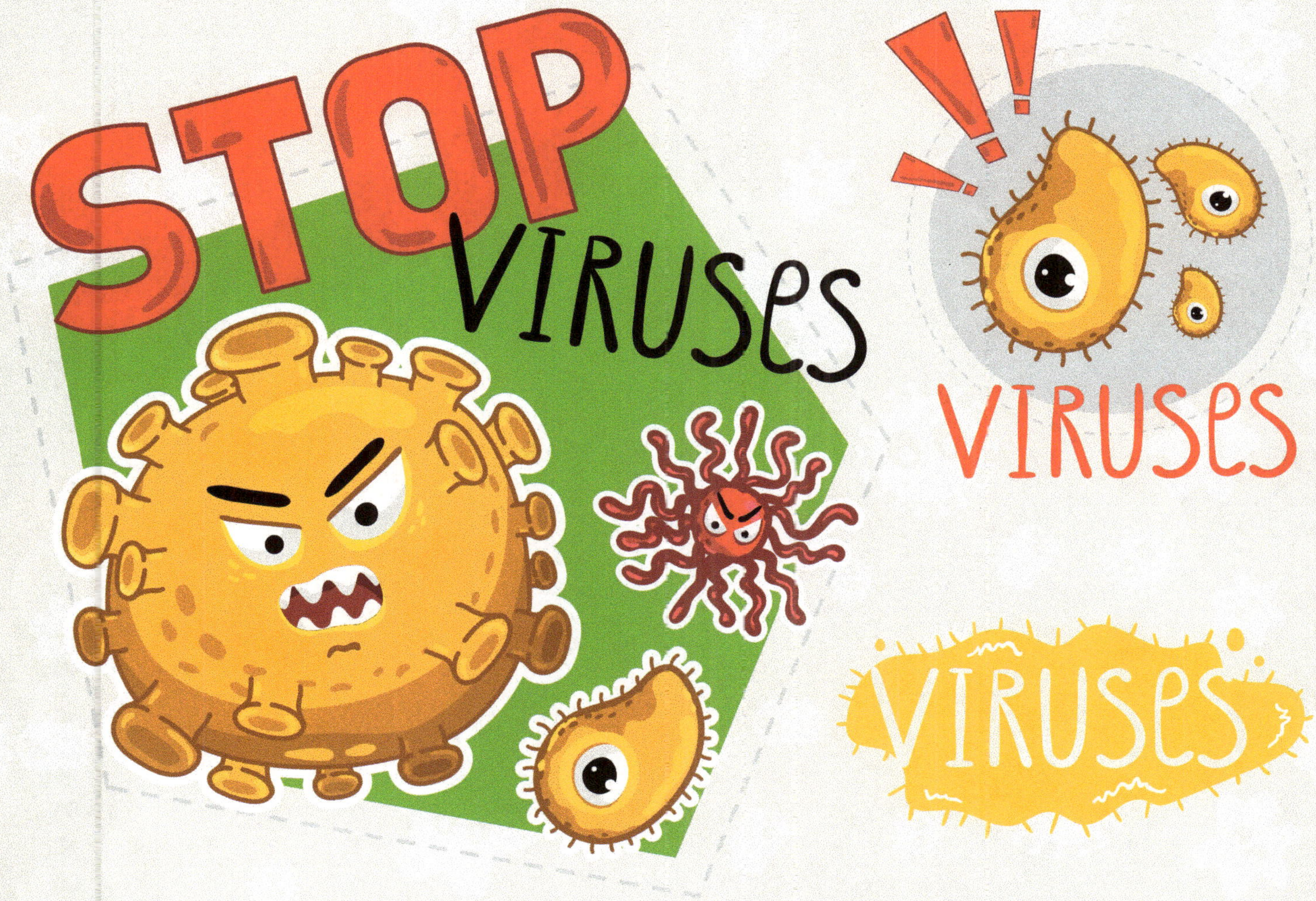

Every year millions of people around the world get sick from the flu virus, and many die.

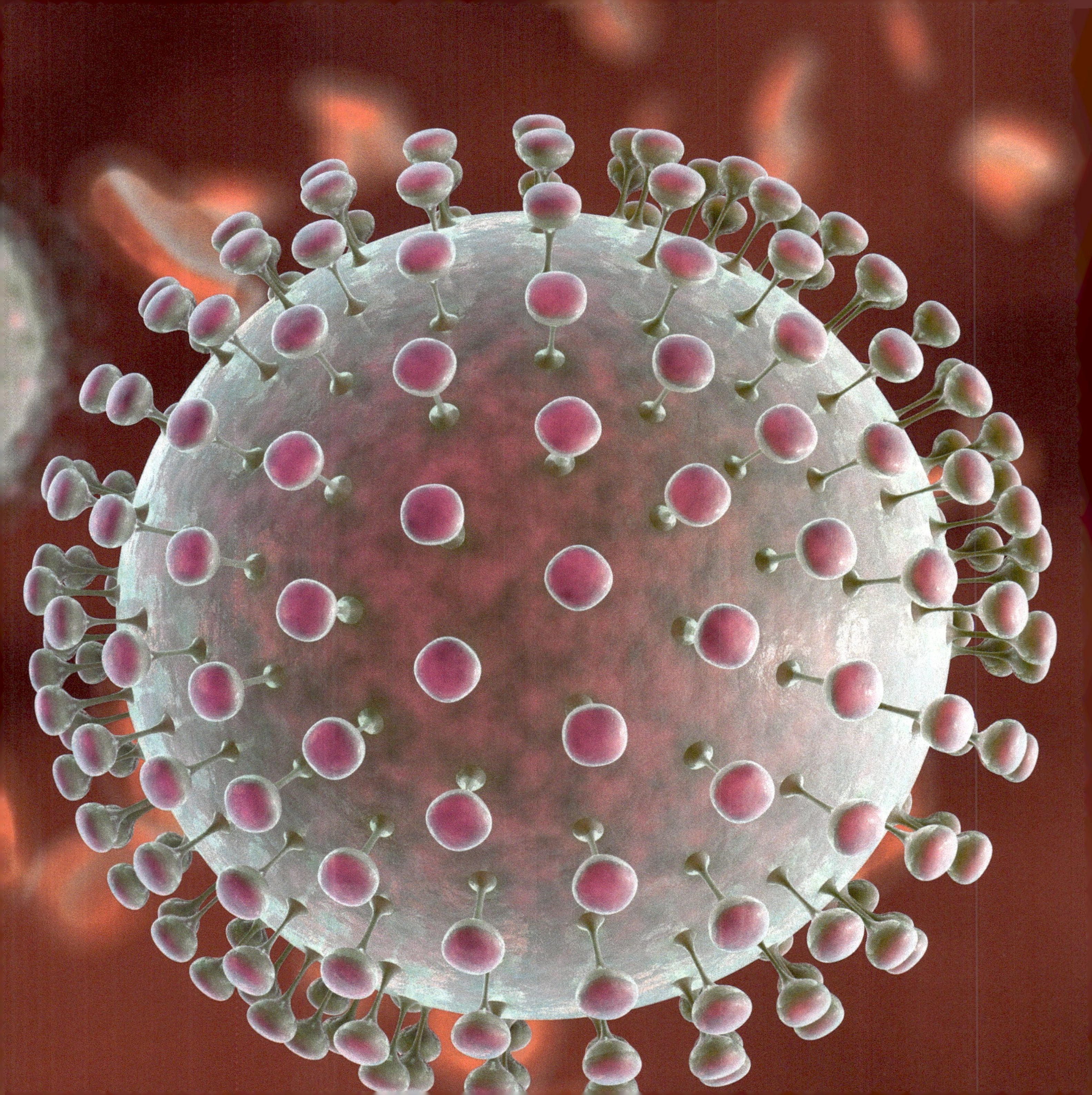

Viruses can hang around on doorknobs, toilet seats, cell phones, and surfaces like the handles of shopping carts for up to two days, waiting for the next host to touch them. If you touch something that has viruses on it, and then put your hand to your mouth, eyes, or nose before you have had a chance to wash your hands, you may transfer those eager viruses into your body.

Zika virus in blood with red blood cells.

keep safe from infections

Having all these disease-carrying things around you, so small you can't see them, sounds pretty scary. Fortunately, there are lots of things you can do to reduce the risk of picking up germs that could make you sick.

Sanitation concept.

sanitizing the baby things
in uv sterilizer and dryer.

SOAP

Wash your hands. a lot!

Since disease-carrying viruses and other microbes can live a long time on surfaces like doorknobs and kitchen tables and your computer keyboard, you have to presume they are getting on your hands quite often. Once there, they just wait for a chance to get in your mouth, nose, ears, or eyes.

Illustration of a person washing their hands with soap and water.

The best and least-expensive defense is to wash your hands frequently with soap and water, or with a disinfecting gel. Just passing your hands through running water does not do the trick! Here's what the Center for Disease Control recommends:

Washing of hands with soap under running water.

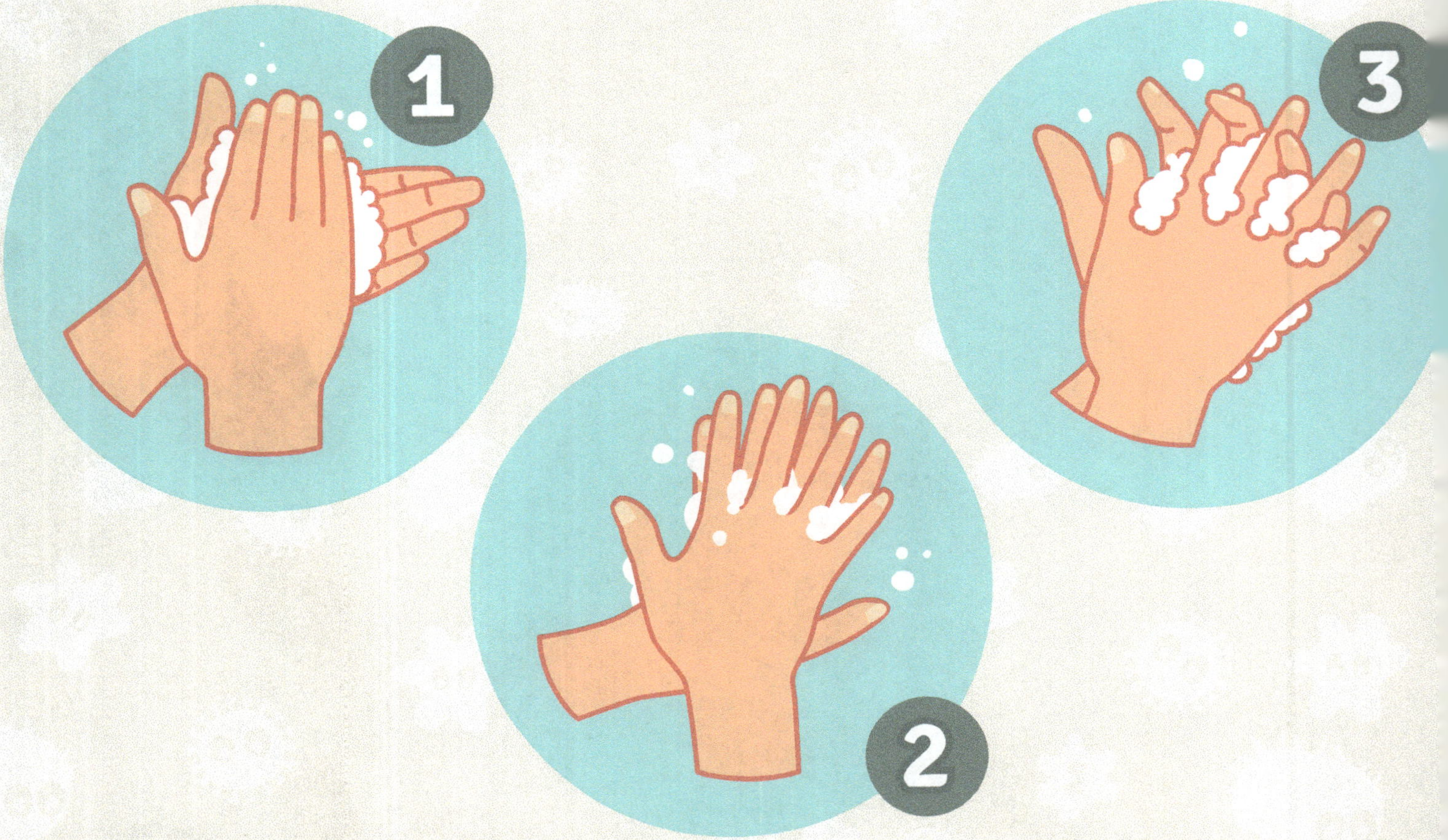

- Wet your hands and put soap on them.
- Wash your hands vigorously in water while you sing “Happy Birthday” to yourself - that will take about twenty seconds.

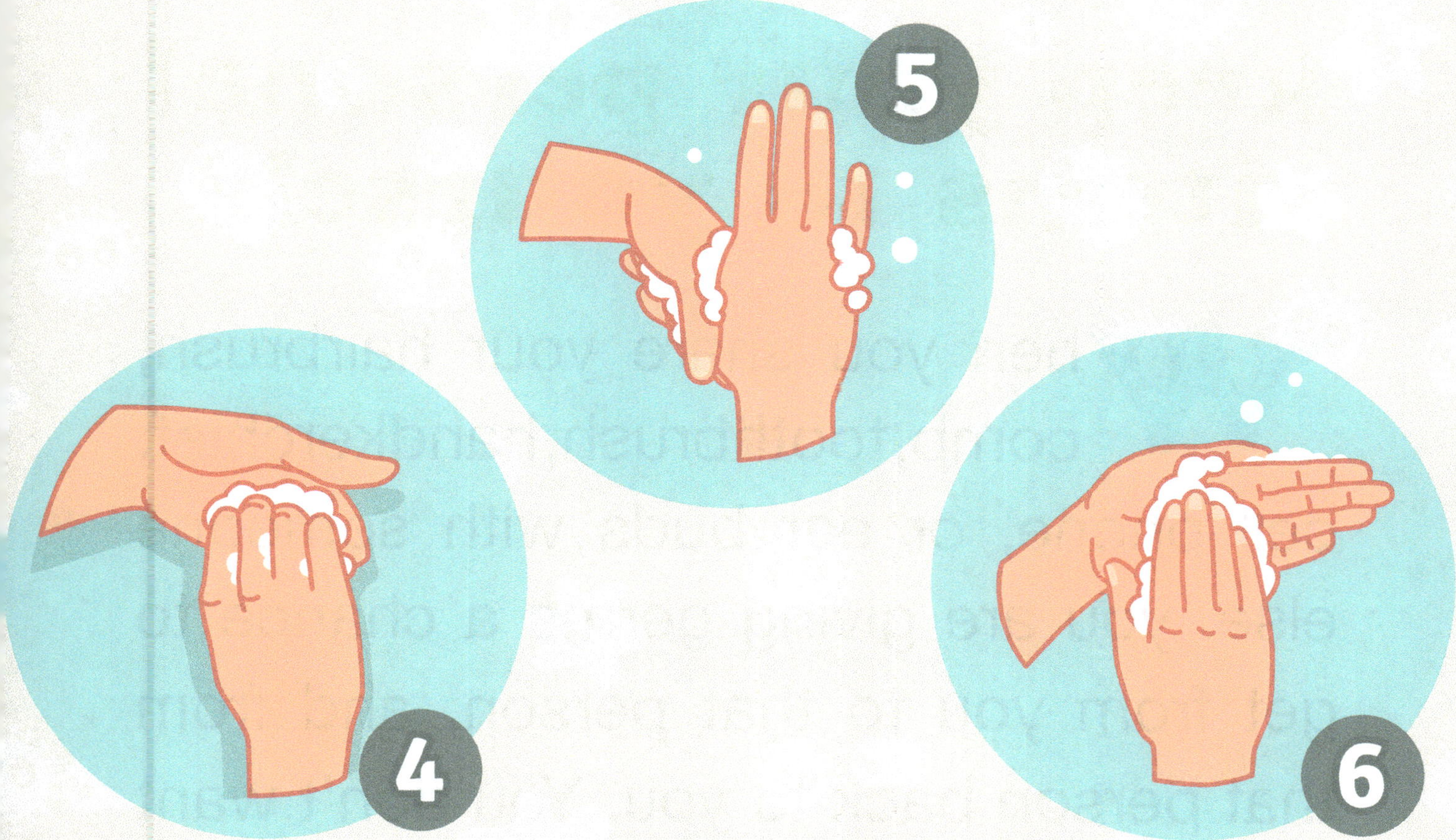

Hands washing medical instructions.

- Dry your hands with a paper towel or a clean towel that nobody else has used. If there is a blow-dry device, as there often is in a public restroom, you can use that.

keep your personal items to yourself

When you share your hairbrush, comb, toothbrush, handkerchief, cell phone, or ear buds with someone else, you are giving germs a chance to get from you to that person, and from that person back to you. You don't want to get sick, right? And you certainly don't want to make somebody else sick. Let your friends get their own combs and ear buds!

Headphones.

toothbrush and tooth
on a wooden floor

cover your mouth before you cough!

People often have germs at work in them while they feel just fine. You have to take care not to pass what you have to other people. When you cough or sneeze, make sure you cover your mouth and nose. A cough is like a germ shotgun, firing tiny droplets of water into the air around you. Each of those droplets can be carrying germs.

Little girl covers her mouth while coughing.

If you have nothing else, cover you mouth and nose with your hand, and then wash your hands immediately. If you are away from a place where you can wash, cover your mouth and nose with your sleeve or your elbow so you don't get germs all over your hands, ready to pass on to the next person you meet.

Boy wipes his nose with a tissue.

Sick kids.

Chef in restaurant kitchen.

be a safe cook

Even if your food seems fresh and your kitchen seems clean, there are microbes and germ-carriers all over the place. Any house fly is happy to land on your kitchen counter, walk around with its dirty feet, and poop a tiny, germ-filled poop!

Lots of people get what they think is a flu, but is really food poisoning caused by germs in the food they eat.

To do your best job as a cook, keep food refrigerated until just before you need it. Keep it covered while it sits on the counter. Wash or peel fruit and vegetables to make sure you are not about to eat what was on the hands of the last person who touched them. Wash your counter and table tops regularly, even if they look clean.

Family cooking.

View from airport terminal.

travel safely

When you travel to another town or another country, you can easily pick up germs that can make you sick. Who sat in that seat in the airport just before you? Who is that person coughing somewhere in the train station or the restaurant?

When you are traveling, one of the key things to make sure of is access to clean water. Even if the local people happily drink the local water, you may not be able to. There may be protozoa your body has never met, carrying germs you do not want. Remember that ice cubes made from local water can have just as many germ carriers as any other water. Find a source of bottled water you can use for drinking and for tooth-brushing.

Bottles of mineral water.

Eat cooked foods, and stay away from raw vegetables and fruits unless you peel them.

If you are traveling overseas, check with your doctor to make sure that your immunizations are up-to-date. There are few things worse for spoiling a vacation than getting sick!

Man using a mask, protecting himself from smog.

no nose-picking!

When you pick your nose, you are getting microbes and germs all over your finger. Unless you wash your hands right away, your finger is now a germ delivery system for the whole world. Avoid passing on the germs you carry to other people, directly or indirectly.

Little baby boy with finger in his nose.

YOUR MYSTERIOUS BODY

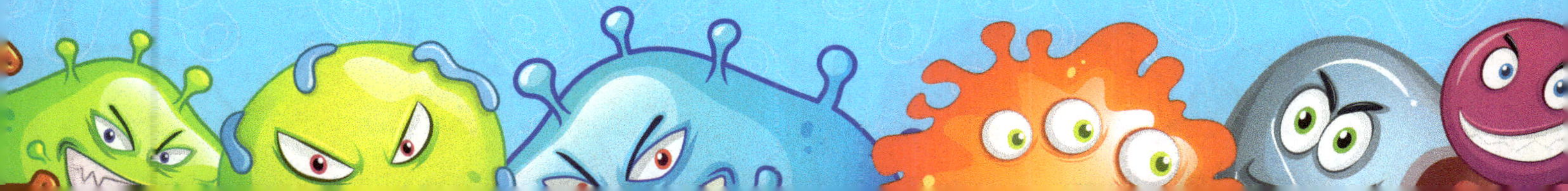

Your body is a tough, complicated, capable system, if you manage to keep it from getting sick. It is worth taking care of your body: when you are healthy you can enjoy the world much more!

Infected water and waterborne disease risk as a human hand holding a drop of contaminated dirty drinking or washing liquid with bacteria viruses.

Learn more about your body in Baby Professor books like I Can See, Hear, Taste, Smell, and Feel! and The Human Brain.

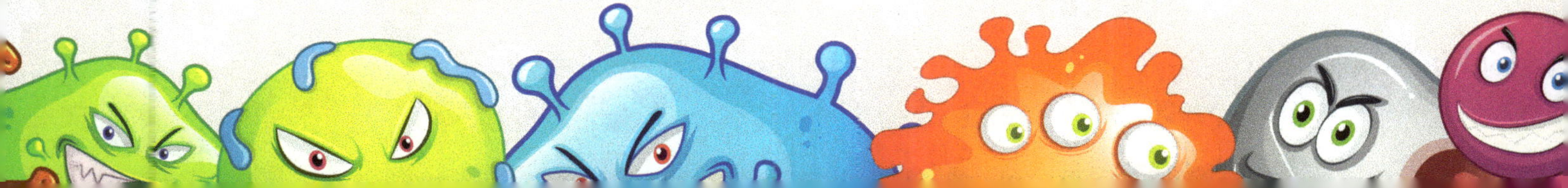

Milton Keynes UK
Ingram Content Group UK Ltd.
UKHW051129030924
447802UK00003B/126

9 798869 415608